Games for Netball Training

Games for Netball Training

Joyce Wheeler

PELHAM BOOKS

First published in Great Britain by
PELHAM BOOKS LTD
44 Bedford Square
London WC1B 3DU
1979

ISBN 0 7207 1162 2

Typeset by Granada Graphics
and printed and bound in Great Britain by
Billing and Sons Ltd., Guildford, London and Worcester

Line drawings by John Levy

Contents

Foreword

by J. Robinson

President of the All England Netball Association

More women than ever are playing and enjoying the game of netball. From this enjoyment grows the desire to improve and hence the need and demand for more coaching. Netball requires disciplined skills from the individual player and only when these basic skills have been acquired can the team tactics be developed. To achieve a reasonable standard in the basics involves coaching sessions which, through necessity, may include repetitive, sometimes tedious activities which can destroy the enthusiasm of those taking part. The contents of this book should help relieve this problem and stimulate interest and enthusiasm.

Miss Wheeler has been England's coach for four years and was the Development Officer of the All England Netball Association for five years. In this capacity she travelled throughout England coaching, advising, helping and talking with netballers of all ages and all levels of ability. She, more than anyone, is in a position to assess the needs of coaches and has made full use of her experience and expertise in her book. It is a welcome addition to the as yet small pool of printed resources for netball.

Introduction

The instructions and rules for each game are explained simply but there are a few general points I should like to make.

1. The A.E.N.A. (All England Netball Association) rules apply and should be enforced, such as free passes, penalty passes and shots, throw-ins, throw-ups. In some games there are a few exceptions to the rules, e.g. the way in which a game is started.
2. The illustrations are meant to give the reader the intentions behind the game and are not necessarily to scale.
3. The games have been divided into specific areas:

1– 5	Warming activities;
6–22	Stamina and fitness training;
23–65	Skills training;
66–81	Tactical training;
82–89	Reaction training;
90–96	Supplementary games.

It is obvious that the emphasis in each game can be changed and many of them can provide training for other aspects of the game. Many of the games in the first three areas overlap and give training in more areas than the one under which they are listed.

The **warming games** are designed to train the body for the explosive and speed movements. In particular, these games provide training for sudden changes of direction and sprinting movements over short distances.

The **stamina and fitness games** demand working under pressure for specific lengths of time. They are aimed to help the player to improve her level of endurance and speed, also her ability to maintain a high standard of play for a considerable period of time, i.e. longer than the time demanded in a full game. The demands made on each individual player must be considered according to her ability and physique. The recovery period between strenuous games should be long enough for the player to be able to perform again efficiently, but the work load given should exert her fully, so that she experiences a feeling of exhaustion.

The **skills training games** are designed to improve the player's level of skill in a realistic situation. Stress should be placed on acquiring correct skills technique and it is important to work towards perfecting accuracy. Skill should not be sacrificed at the expense of speed. Once the player achieves a good level of skill, then she should be asked to use her skills under pressure, i.e. by introducing increased speed into the game.

The **tactical games** obviously bring in simple tactical moves. These games teach the player to learn to select and use the correct skill at the appropriate time and emphasize the importance of working with other players, if a successful move is to result.

As each game is played in a small area and at a high speed, players' reactions need to be good. The amount of recovery time is brief, so the **reaction training games** are included to speed up reaction time.

The **supplementary games** are included to improve the general skills and fitness of the player. They introduce an element of relaxation.

Obviously there are many other games which could be included in this book but it is hoped that those given might start you thinking. There are many adaptations which can be made and no doubt you will be able to add to them.

Game 1

Purpose:	Warming up
No. of players:	In twos
Playing area:	Approx. 5m × 5m
Duration:	5 minutes
Outline:	Two players face one another approximately 1m apart. On a signal one player tries to tread on the other player's toes. Count the number of times successful.
Rules:	(1) Players must remain facing each other. (2) No bodily contact.
Variations:	(1) Restricting the playing area. (2) On the whistle the players change task.

Game 2

Purpose:	Warming up
No. of players:	In groups of 3
Playing area:	10m × 8m
Duration:	5 minutes
Outline:	Two players face each other and join hands. The third player stands behind one of the two players. The third player tries to touch the player who is furthest away. Count the number of touches made in the set time.
Rules:	Attacking player may not contact the interposing player in her effort to touch the target.
Variation:	After a given number of touches the players change over.

Game 3

Purpose:	Warming up and skills training (footwork)
No. of players:	In groups of 4
Playing area:	Approx. 10m × 8m
Duration:	5 minutes
Outline:	Three players join hands and form a circle; the fourth player outside the circle, faces one of the three players. The fourth player must touch the player opposite as many times as possible in the given time.
Rules:	Attacking player must not contact the other players in her effort to reach her target – she must go round the outside of the circle and not lean across it.
Variation:	The outside player must touch a given part of the body, e.g. shoulder, arm, middle of the back.

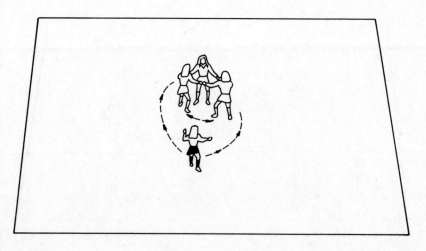

Game 4

Purpose: Warming up and space awareness
No. of players: In twos
Playing area: A netball court or larger area
Duration: 3-5 minutes
Outline: In twos, numbered 1 and 2. Starting side by side, on the command 'go' No.1 sprints into a space as far away from No.2 as possible. On the word 'stop' No.1 stops; on the word 'go' No.2 sprints and tries to touch No.1 before receiving the command 'stop'. Count the number of times the chasing player touches.

Rules: The chaser must not move until she is told.
Variations: (1) Speed up the game – the coach blowing a whistle to stop and start the players, i.e. No.1 stops, No.2 runs, etc. (2) No.1 must change direction before sprinting.

Remarks: The player running into a space should be trained not to do so until she is sure it is free.

14

Game 5

Purpose:	Warming up and ball handling
No. of players:	In twos
Playing area:	Any small area on a netball court
Duration:	5 minutes
Outline:	In twos, facing each other, one player with the ball. Player with the ball keeps possession by bouncing the ball with one or two hands. The other player tries to get possession.
Rules:	(1) Players may move freely but must remain facing each other. (2) Players may not catch the ball.
Variations:	(1) Limit the hand used for bouncing. (2) Allow the player with the ball to move freely, i.e. making it unnecessary for the players to keep facing one another.

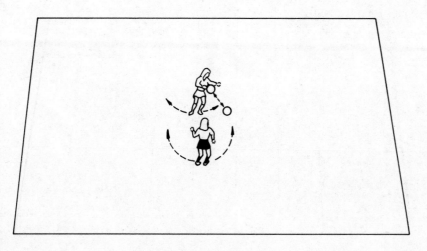

Game 6

Purpose:	Stamina training and footwork
No. of players:	Any number
Playing area:	The length of a netball court. Additional lines 3m apart
Duration:	5 minutes
Outline:	Individual shuttle runs. Starting behind the goal line each player runs to the first line touches it with her hand, turns and returns to the start. Then she runs to the second line and returns to the start. The number of times this is repeated depends on the ability of the group.
Rules:	Scoring: (1) Number of repetitions in the given time. (2) First player to complete the run.
Variations:	(1) Touching the line with the right/left hand or foot. (2) Running sideways, backwards, hopping, leaping, etc.
Remarks:	The number of shuttles should be limited according to the ability of the group, gradually working up to using the whole length of the court (30.5m).

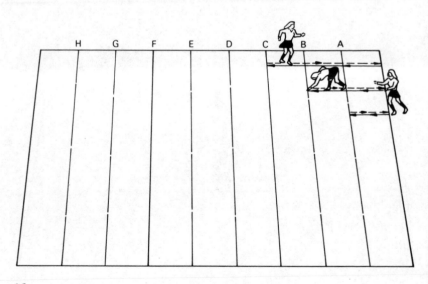

Game 7

Purpose:	Stamina training
No. of players:	Any number
Playing area:	Length of the court. Additional lines 3m apart
Duration:	5 minutes or more
Outline:	Individual shuttle runs. Each player runs to the first line, 'A', turns and goes back to the start. Next she runs to line 'B' and returns to line 'A'. Then she runs to line 'C', returning to line 'B', and so on. This continues until the runner arrives at the end of the court or the target set by the coach.
Rules:	As in Game 6.
Variations:	As in Game 6.

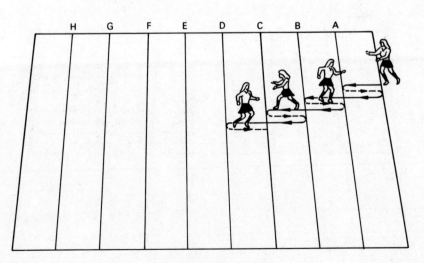

Game 8

Purpose:	Stamina training
No. of players:	Any number
Playing area:	Length of the court
Duration:	5-10 minutes
Outline:	As in Game 6 but each player runs the length of a third of the court, turns and runs back to the start. She then runs to the two-thirds line, returns to the start and sprints to the opposite goal line.
Rules:	As in Game 6.
Variations:	As in Game 6.

Game 9

Purpose:	Stamina training
No. of players:	Any number
Playing area:	Length of court
Duration:	5 minutes
Outline:	As in Game 6 but the player runs to the first third line, returns to the start, runs to the second third line, turns, runs back to the first third line, turns, runs to the goal line, turns, runs back to the second third line, turns, and sprints to the goal line.
Rules:	As in Game 6.
Variations:	As in Game 6.

Game 10

Purpose:	Stamina training
No. of players:	Any number, in pairs
Playing area:	The length of the court. Additional lines approx. 3m apart
Duration:	5 minutes
Outline:	Shuttle runs in twos, as in Game 7. Player No.1 sprints to line 'A' and back to the start, touches No.2 and both players run – No.1 going to line 'B', No.2 going to line 'A'. This continues until both players arrive at the opposite goal line.
Rules:	Players may overtake one another.
Variations:	As in Game 6.

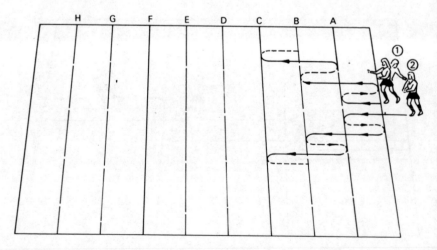

Game 11

Purpose:	Stamina training
No. of players:	Teams of 3-7 or more
Playing area:	5m × 15m
Duration:	5-8 minutes
Outline:	Divide the team in half and start approximately 15m apart in single file. The thrower passes the ball to the opposite player and runs to the end of the opposite team. The catcher runs forward, catches the ball and passes to the player facing and then finishes by running to the back of the opposite team. Count the number of circuits completed.
Rules:	Receiving player uses a running pass.
Variations:	(1) State the pass to be used. (2) Players use twenty chest passes then twenty underarm passes.

21

Game 12

Purpose:	Stamina and skills training
No. of players:	Teams of 3-7 or more
Playing area:	15m × 5m
Duration:	5-10 minutes
Outline:	Divide each team in half and in lines approximately 15m apart facing one another. A player from one side runs forward, receives the ball in the centre from the first member of the opposing team, pivots, throws to the next member of her own side, then turns and runs to the end of the opposite team. Count the number of successful passes made in the set time.
Rules:	The player passing to the moving player uses a shoulder pass, the one passing from the centre uses a two-handed pass.
Variations:	(1) Alter the pass used. (2) Vary the footwork used in the centre, i.e. turn to face the direction of the next throw, making the turn in the air while catching the ball (advanced players).

Game 13

Purpose:	Stamina training
No. of players:	Teams of 4-7
Playing area:	Width of court, approx. 15m
Duration:	5-8 minutes
Outline:	The teams are divided into two halves, each half starting beyond the side lines. The first member of one team throws the ball to the first member of the opposite team who sprints forward to receive the ball. The catcher pivots and throws to the next player in her team. She returns to the back of her team. Winners – the team who complete the activity the most times in the time allowed.
Rules:	Players use the shoulder pass.
Variations:	(1) Alter the pass used. (2) Change the pass when the ball is back with the first player. (3) Winners – the team with highest number of successful passes.
Remarks:	Where there is an odd number in a team, the side with the smaller number of players start with the ball.

Game 14

Purpose:	Stamina training
No. of players:	Groups of 9, divided 4:5
Playing area:	A third of the court
Duration:	5-10 minutes
Outline:	The team of five keep possession of the ball with the team of four marking.
Rules:	(1) The players are free to move in their playing area. (2) The team of five score a point each time they successfully get a pass to their unmarked player. (3) The attacking team get as many points as possible in the set time. Then the teams change with the odd player joining the team of four.
Variations:	(1) Limit the pass used, e.g. shoulder, chest, underarm, two-handed. (2) State the type of dodge to be used, e.g. change of direction, sudden stop. (3) Count the passes made from the odd player to the marked player.

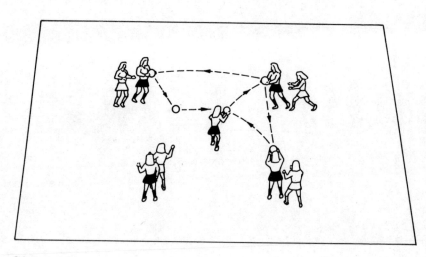

Game 15

Purpose:	Stamina training
No. of players:	Groups of 9 divided into two teams of 4, plus an 'extra' player
Playing area:	Half a third of the court 10m × 8m
Duration:	5-10 minutes
Outline:	As in Game 14. The playing area is divided into three sections, approximately 3.5m each. Two players from each team play in the two outer areas while the 'extra' player works in the central area against both teams. The teams pass across to their other two players, the 'extra' player trying to intercept the pass. The teams score a point for each successful pass made.
Rules:	When the 'extra' player intercepts, she changes with the player who threw the ball.
Variations:	(1) Limit the number of passes allowed in each area before passing to the rest of the team. (2) Limit the pass and dodge used.

Game 16

Purpose:	Stamina training and space awareness
No. of players:	Groups of 7-9
Playing area:	Half a third of the court 10m × 8m
Duration:	5-10 minutes
Outline:	Each group is divided 4:3 or 4:5. The larger team play just inside the area; the smaller team in the middle. The outer team keep possession of the ball, moving freely in the playing area. The smaller team try to intercept.
Rules:	(1) A player who intercepts changes places with the thrower. (2) Players score a point for each interception. (3) Winner is the first player to score 3 points or to make the highest number of interceptions in the set time.
Variation:	Limit the type of pass used.

Game 17

Purpose:	Stamina training and space marking
No. of players:	Teams of 7 divided 4:3
Playing area:	10m × 10m
Duration:	5-10 minutes
Outline:	As in Game 16 but the positions reversed, i.e. the larger side in the middle. The smaller side start with the ball and moving freely keep possession. The larger side try to intercept.
Rules:	(1) When an interception is made the sides change places, with the intercepting side keeping possession. (2) The ball and the players must stay in their area. (3) To score, count the number of interceptions made.
Remarks:	The same game can be played with the emphasis placed on the attacking team and scoring based on the number of accurate passes.

Game 18

Purpose:	Stamina training
No. of players:	Teams of 5 or more
Playing area:	10m × 10m
Duration:	10 minutes
Outline:	The players form a circle with one player in the centre with the ball. The centre player passes to any other player who moves into a space to receive the ball. The centre player then takes the place of one of the circle players who then moves to receive the next pass.
Rules:	(1) A player may not throw to the player from whom she has just received the ball. (2) She may not return to her original position immediately. (3) Count the number of passes. (4) The team try to get the highest number of passes in the set time.
Variation:	Vary the pass used.

Game 19

Purpose:	Stamina training
No. of players:	Two teams of 5
Playing area:	Half the court
Duration:	10-15 minutes
Outline:	The court is divided through the centre circle. An extra post is put on the side line where it joins the centre-third line.
	Both teams try to score as many goals as possible. The game starts with a throw-up between two players in the centre area.
Rules:	(1) Players may score in either goal. (2) Any player may shoot. (3) Only one attempt to shoot allowed in one goal by the same team. (4) Four passes must be made between attempts to shoot.
Variations:	(1) Increase the number of passes between goals. (2) The position of the extra post may be changed.

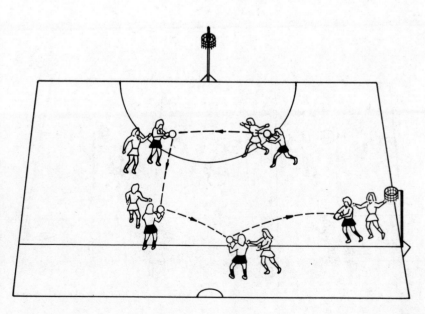

Game 20

Purpose:	Stamina training
No. of players:	Two teams of 7
Playing area:	A netball court
Duration:	10-15 minutes
Outline:	The goal posts are moved to the front of the shooting circle. Each team tries to score as many goals as possible.
Rules:	(1) Each team shoots into a different goal. (2) The game starts with a throw-up between any two players in the centre third. (3) Players are allowed to move freely about the court, i.e. no offside rule. (4) Any player may shoot from any position on the court. (5) The game is continuous – after a goal has been scored the retrieving team continue the game.
Variations:	(1) Set a number of passes which must be made before players are allowed to shoot. (2) After a goal, re-start the game with a throw-up in the centre (this gives practice for this skill).

Game 21

Purpose:	Stamina training
No. of players:	Two teams of any number
Playing area:	A netball court
Duration:	15-20 minutes
Outline:	A bench is placed at each end of the court at the front of the goal circle. The players divide into two equal teams. One member from each team stands on the bench. Each team passing the ball tries to throw the ball to their player on the form.
Rules:	(1) No offside rule. (2) The player on the form is allowed to move freely along the bench. (3) The game starts with a throw-up between two players in the centre third. (4) A point is scored for each pass received by the player on the bench. This player must remain in contact with the bench whilst she has the ball.
Variation:	Limit the number of passes or type of pass used.
Remarks:	Make the playing periods short, as this is a strenuous game.

Game 22

Purpose:	Stamina and speed training
No. of players:	Teams of 4-6
Playing area:	10m × 15m
Duration:	5-10 minutes
Outline:	Two teams, A and B: team A sprinting in relay round their area; team B passing the ball, i.e. chest then shoulder pass. Players in set formation.
Order of passes:	Team of 4: 1 to 2 shoulder pass, 2 to 3 chest pass, 3 to 4 shoulder pass, 4 to 1 chest pass.
	Team of 6: Chest pass in order 1 to 6 and then reverse order back to 1.
Rules:	Teams try to complete their activity as many times as possible in the given time.
Variations:	(1) Vary the passes. (2) Sprinting team vary their step, e.g. sideways, hopping.

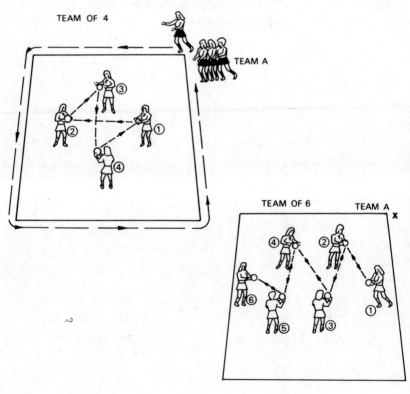

Game 23

Purpose: Skills training (footwork) and warming up
No. of players: Groups of 3-4, or more
Playing area: 10m × 15m
Duration: 3-5 minutes
Outline: One player has the ball and keeps possession by
                bouncing it. The other players try to gain
                possession and continue bouncing the ball.
Rules: (1) Players may not catch the ball. (2) All players
                may move freely in their playing area.
Variations: (1) Limit the hand used, i.e. both, right or left. (2)
                Limit the playing area. (3) See how many times
                one player can get the ball in the given time.

Game 24

Purpose:	Skills training (footwork) and warming up
No. of players:	Teams of 4-5
Playing area:	Width of the court (15m approx.)
Duration:	3-5 minutes
Outline:	In single file, players approximately 1m apart. The leader zig-zags in and out of the team until she arrives back in her original position. The next player in the line then takes her turn, and so on until all players have had a turn.
Rules:	(1) Players must run to the front of the team first. (2) No bodily contact is allowed by the runner.
Variations:	(1) Running backwards, remembering to turn the head towards the way you are turning. (2) Bouncing a ball at the same time. (3) Using slip steps.
Remarks:	Emphasis should be made on using small continuous steps to get through the gaps.

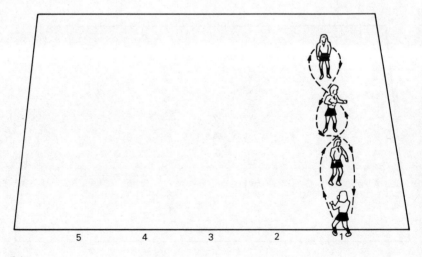

Game 25

Purpose:	Skills training (footwork) and warming up
No. of players:	Teams of 4-5
Playing area:	Width of the court
Duration:	3-5 minutes
Outline:	As in Game 24, but here the game is progressive with all players moving. As No.1 passes No.2, No.2 follows on behind and they continue 'picking up' players as they move up the line. When No.1 reaches the last player in the team, she runs past and stops approximately 1m in front of her. The other players continue in this way until the last player arrives at the head of the line. This player then turns round and starts back down the team picking-up players until all have returned to their original positions.
Rules:	No bodily contact is allowed by runners.
Variation:	Move backwards on the return run.

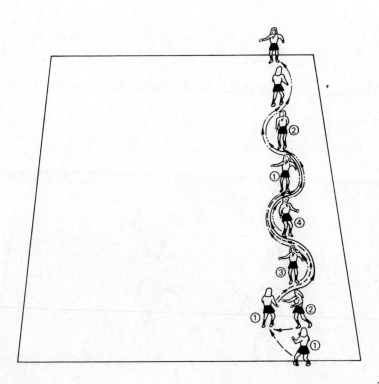

Game 26

Purpose:	Skills training (footwork) and warming up
No. of players:	Teams of 6 or more
Playing area:	Approx. 10m × 8m
Duration:	5 minutes
Outline:	Players in a circle and numbered 1 to 6. No.1 starts zig-zagging in and out of the other players. When she gets to No.3, No.6 starts chasing No.1 and tries to touch her before she gets back to her starting place. No.2 then sets off and the same sequence takes place.
Rules:	(1) The players in the circle remain stationary until their turn. (2) The zig-zagging player may not contact the other players.
Variations:	(1) The coach calls a number and that player tries to get home before the player two places away catches her. (2) The coach calls two numbers, the first-called player tries to get home without being touched by the second-called player.

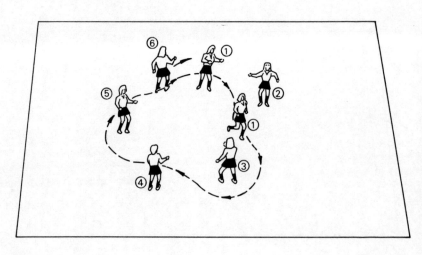

Game 27

Purpose:	Skills training (changing direction quickly)
No. of players:	In groups of 2 or 3
Playing area:	Width of the netball court
Duration:	3–5 minutes
Outline:	The players start behind a side line and jog towards the opposite line; at any time one selected player turns and sprints for the starting line. The other player(s) try and beat her over the starting line.
Rules:	The winner is the player who gets both feet over the starting line first.
Variations:	(1) The players jog towards line 'B' and then sprint over line 'B'. (2) The players sprint towards 'B' and the selected player chooses whether she returns to line 'A' or 'B'. (3) Stipulate the method of turning, e.g. with a pivot; with continuous steps; with swivel-turning the feet on the spot and transferring weight to the front foot. (4) Changing turning direction.

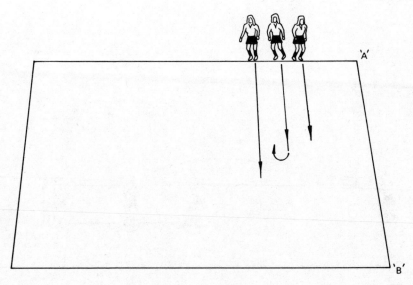

Game 28

Purpose:	Skills training (footwork)
No. of players:	In twos, or small teams (fours)
Playing area:	15m × 5m approx.
Duration:	3-5 minutes
Outline:	In twos, facing one another approximately 10m apart. (If in fours, one player facing the other three in a single file.) A line of varying-sized circles are spaced evenly between the two players. One player passes the ball to her partner who must catch the ball in each circle in order. The player receiving the ball in the circle passes it back to the thrower. When she gets to the last circle she keeps the ball and goes to the front of the line. The thrower runs to the starting position and the activity is repeated. If playing in a small team, the thrower goes to the back of the team and the next player starts. The winners are the first team to finish.
Rules:	(1) The catching player must receive the ball wholly in the circle. (2) She must jump to land in each circle and not be grounded to catch the ball.
Variation:	Indicate the type of footwork to be used, e.g. landing on two feet, on the right/left foot.
Remarks:	The size of the circles may vary according to the skill of the players.

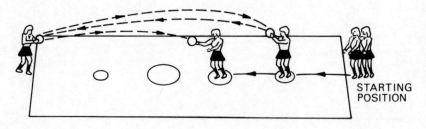

STARTING POSITION

Game 29

Purpose:	Skills training (catching)
No. of players:	In twos
Playing area:	Width of the court, players 3m apart
Duration:	3 minutes
Outline:	One player has the ball and faces forward. She turns, passes the ball to her partner, then runs past her and receives the ball again. This continues until both players are over the side line.
Rules:	(1) The players use a chest pass. (2) Count the number of completed runs (i.e. there and back) made in 3 minutes.
Variations:	(1) Vary the pass used, e.g. bounce, underarm, two-handed. (2) Alternate the side to which the players run. (3) The first pair to complete one run earns a point.

Game 30

Purpose: Skills training under pressure (passing and catching)

No. of players: Teams of 4-7

Playing area: A third of the court

Duration: 5-8 minutes

Outline: One player has the ball; the rest are divided into two teams 15m apart. The player with the ball is positioned halfway between the two teams and on the third line of the court. The ball is passed to each player in turn, running to the centre alternately from each side. When the ball is caught by the running player she returns it to the feeder, then continues running to the back of the opposite team.

Rules: (1) Short pass to be used, i.e. underarm/two-handed. (2) Count the number of accurate passes made in 5 minutes.

Variations: (1) Alter the pass. (2) Count the number of complete circuits.

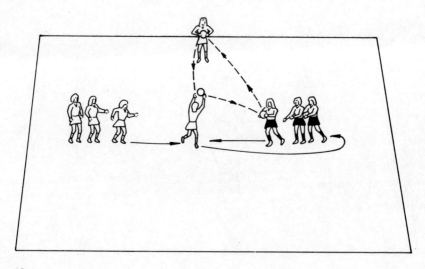

Game 31

Purpose: Skills training (defending)
No. of players: Teams of 4-7
Playing area: A third of the court
Duration: 5-10 minutes
Outline: As in Game 30 but two teams at each side line; one team attacking, the other defending. The player running to receive the pass is marked by a defending player.
Rules: Count the number of times the defending player touches or intercepts the pass in the given time.
Variation: The emphasis is on the attacking player and points are scored by the number of successful passes.
Remarks: Attacking and defending team change over; the teams add together the points they scored when attacking and defending.

Game 32

Purpose:	Skills training
No. of players:	Teams of 4-7
Playing area:	One third of the court.
Duration:	5-8 minutes
Outline:	As in Game 30. Slight variation – the player receiving the ball from the feeder does a running pass to the player facing her. This player passes to the feeder and runs to receive the ball in the centre.
Rules:	Count the number of complete circuits in the set time.

Game 33

Purpose: Skills training (dodging)
No. of players: Teams of 3
Playing area: 10m × 10m
Duration: 10 minutes
Outline: Three against three. The teams try to maintain possession of the ball for ten consecutive passes.
Rules: (1) Players move to receive the ball. (2) Passes must be one short followed by one long. (3) If the ball is intercepted, the team losing possession retain their score.
Variations: (1) After a team lose possession their score reverts to nought (advanced players). (2) Alter the sequence of passes used. (3) After a player has passed the ball she must touch the nearest line to her before returning to the game.

43

Game 34

Purpose:	Skills and speed training
No. of players:	Teams of 3-7
Playing area:	A third of the court
Duration:	3-5 minutes
Outline:	Two equal teams. Team A in single file at one corner of the area. Team B divided into two lines facing one another 5m apart, in the centre of the area (if a team of three, then players form a triangle). The players should be at least an arm's length apart.
Rules:	(1) Team A – a shuttle run: No.1 runs outside the area and touches No.2. She then runs round. This continues until all members of the team have completed their run, then No.1 calls 'stop'. (2) Team B: Starting at No.1 players pass in order across the line using a chest pass. When the ball gets back to No.1 they score a point. Count the number of times the activity is completed. (3) Teams change places and try to beat the opposing team's score.
Variations:	(1) Team A – change the method of getting round, e.g. sideways, hopping, skipping, leaping, etc. (2) Team B – use a different pass.

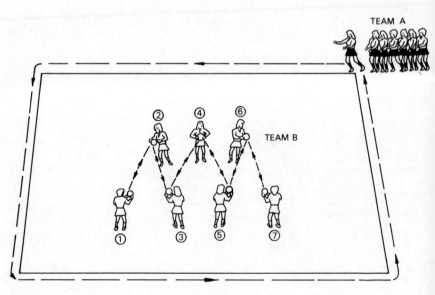

TEAM A

TEAM B

44

Game 35

Purpose:	Skills training (shooting)
No. of players:	In twos
Playing area:	10m × 10m
Duration:	5 minutes
Outline:	As many extra goal posts as possible. Using approximately half the shooting area with a goal post, one player acting as feeder outside the area passes to the other player, who runs forward, catches and shoots. The shooter retrieves the ball and passes back to the other player.
Rules:	(1) The shooter must land in the playing area. (2) After passing, the feeder changes her position out of court. (3) Players change positions when 10 goals have been scored.
Variations:	(1) State the type of shot, i.e. static, step-around, running. (2) The shooter has to receive the ball at a numbered spot. Numbers 1-10 are marked anywhere in the circle. (3) Shooter progresses in order, i.e. 1 to 2 to 3, etc. (4) Shooter has one attempt from each spot, and has only ten shots. (5) Shooter may not move on to the next number until she has scored. She must return to the beginning between each attempt (advanced players).
Remarks:	The number of goals to be scored in the given time should be set according to the skill of the group.

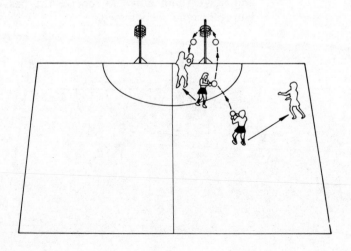

Game 36

Purpose:	Skills training (shooting)
No. of players:	Teams of 5
Playing area:	The circle area
Duration:	5-10 minutes
Outline:	Each team positioned as follows: three players spread around the outside of the circle; two players within the circle. Player No.1, outside the circle, passes the ball round the circle. When the ball reaches No.3 she passes to the nearest circle player (No.4) who moves forward to take the catch. She then passes to the other circle player (No.5) who is moving towards the post to shoot. As soon as No.3 has passed the ball into the circle she moves behind the goal line to retrieve the shot. After each pass the thrower moves on a place. The shooter (No.5) becomes the first outer circle player (replacing No.1), No.1 moves to No.2's position, No.2 to No.3, No.3 moves into the circle as No.4, and No.4 moves to No.5's position and shoots. After retrieving the shot, No.3 passes to No.5 so that the game can start again.
Rules:	(1) The team to score the most goals in the set time are the winners. (2) The first circle player pivots after receiving the ball. (3) The three outer circle players use an underarm pass.
Variations:	(1) Alter the pass used by the three outer players and make them move to receive the pass. (2) Limit the type of shot used.

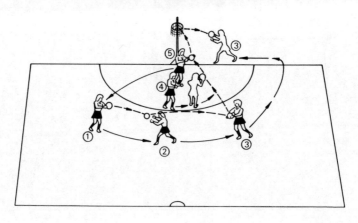

46

Game 37

Purpose:	Skills training (passing/shooting)
No. of players:	In twos
Playing area:	10m × 8m
Duration:	5 minutes
Equipment:	A target e.g. square on the wall or netball post
Outline:	One player passes the ball to her partner (who is approximately 2m away) who then turns and aims at the target/post. The aiming player retrieves the ball and passes it to her partner.
Rules:	(1) The player scores a point for each goal. (2) When a total of 5 points is reached the players change places. (3) The aiming player must use a pivot on turning. (4) Winners are the first pair to score 10 points.
Variations:	(1) The feeding player uses a specific type of pass. (2) If aiming at a target, stipulate the throw to be used. (3) Vary the kind of shot i.e. static or running.

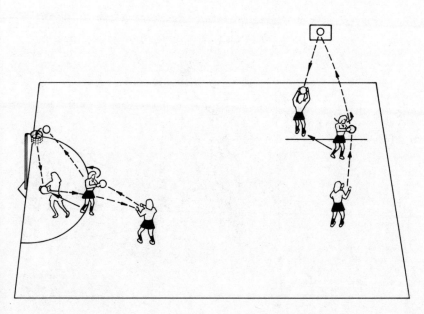

Game 38

Purpose:	Skills training under pressure
No. of players:	Teams of 3
Playing area:	A third of the court (10m × 15m)
Duration:	5 minutes
Outline:	This is a progression from Game 37. Player No.1 passes to No.2 who receives the ball in the circle, then turns and shoots. Player No.3, positioned behind the goal line, retrieves the ball then passes to No.1 who shoots; this time No.2 retrieves the ball. As soon as No.3 has passed the ball she runs to the starting line.
Rules:	(1) Players use a shoulder pass. (2) The first team to score 10 goals are the winners.
Variations:	(1) Vary the type of pass. (2) Limit the kind of shot, i.e. running or static. (3) The team scoring the highest number of goals in the time allowed are the winners.
Remarks:	If there are insufficient goal posts, the groups can practise aiming at a given target.

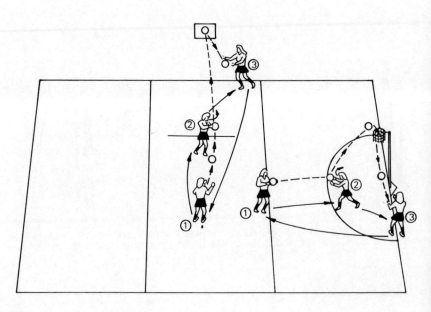

Game 39

Purpose:	Skills training (shooting)
No. of players:	Minimum of three teams of 5
Playing area:	Two-thirds of the court
Duration:	10-15 minutes
Outline:	Starting in the centre the teams pass the ball between them, finally getting it into the circle.
Rules:	(1) The players are numbered 1 to 5. Both teams shoot into the same goal. (2) Each player must receive the ball in a shooting position and this must be done in order, i.e. first attempt at the goal must be made by No.1. (3) The shooter must be in the circle to score. (4) After a missed shot, if the ball is still in play, it must be passed back to the two-thirds line before working back to the goal. The same rule applies for a throw-in. (5) If a goal is scored the game is started again by a centre pass taken alternately.
Variations:	(1) Every player must receive the ball before the correct-numbered player shoots. (2) A set number of passes to be made before the shooter may shoot.

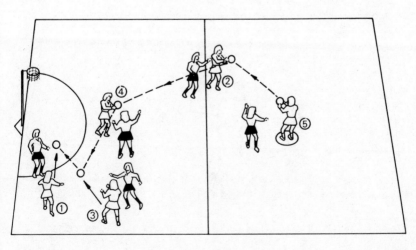

Game 40

Purpose:	Skills and speed training
No. of players:	In teams of 4-7
Playing area:	10m × 10m approx.
Duration:	5 minutes
Outline:	Players in a circle with one player in the centre. A player from the circle starts with the ball and passes to the centre player and moves into the centre. Centre player passes to the next player in the circle and then goes to the free place in the circle.
Rules:	(1) Players use a chest pass. (2) After one complete circuit the players pass in the opposite direction. (3) Count the number of successful circuits in the given time. Alternatively (4) the first team to achieve a set number of circuits can be the winners.
Variation:	Vary the type of pass.

Game 41

Purpose: Skills, speed and reaction training
No. of players: Teams of 5-7
Playing area: 10m × 10m
Duration: 5 minutes
Outline: Players in a circle. Players pass the ball across the circle to one another. As soon as the player has thrown the ball she runs to take up the position of the player to whom she has thrown.
Rules: (1) Players use the shoulder pass. (2) The pass must go across the area. (3) The thrower aims to get to the catcher before she releases the ball. (4) Count the number of successful passes.

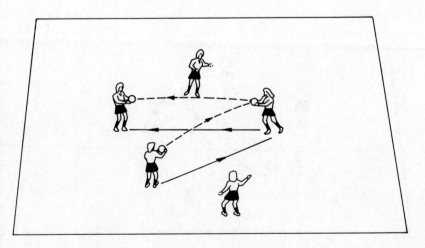

Game 42

Purpose:	Skills, speed and reaction training
No. of players:	Teams of 5-7 or more
Playing area:	10m × 10m approx.
Duration:	5-10 minutes
Outline:	As in Game 41 but after throwing the ball the player runs to intercept the next pass.
Rules:	As in Game 41 except that (1) a player scores a point on each interception. (2) On an interception the player passes the ball back to the thrower and rejoins the circle.
Variation:	Players use an underarm/bounce pass to avoid the defending player.

Game 43

Purpose:	Skills, stamina and spatial training
No. of players:	Teams of 3 or more
Playing area:	15m × 10m
Duration:	5-10 minutes
Outline:	Each team, numbered 1-3, tries to keep possession of the ball for a given time or a specific number of passes.
Rules:	(1) Each team must pass in order and stay in their area. (2) Players may move freely. (3) Players use a sprint dodge to receive the ball. (4) Count the number of successful passes made using the correct dodge to do so.
Variations:	(1) Limit the pass used. (2) Vary the dodge. (3) Only count consecutive successful passes.
Remarks:	Once a player has passed the ball she must move away, thus leaving space for the third member of the team.

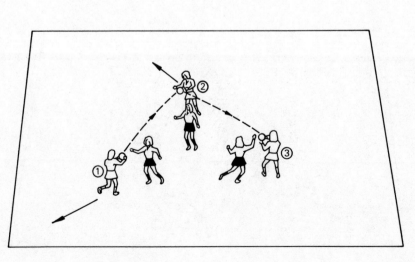

Game 44

Purpose:	Skills, stamina and spatial training
No. of players:	Teams of 3
Playing area:	10m × 15m
Duration:	5-10 minutes
Outline:	The players number 1 to 3. Each team keeps possession of the ball by passing to the other members of the team who move freely to receive the ball. The player with the ball calls a number and that player moves to receive the pass.
Rules:	(1) The pass must go to the player called. (2) The pass must be received in the playing area. (3) The players use a change of direction dodge to receive the ball.
Remarks:	This game trains for the thrower to move away after her pass and leave the space either for the third player or for herself, depending on the number called. The thrower must wait to pass until she sees where the receiver is going.

Game 45

Purpose:	Skills training (passing)
No. of players:	In teams of 5-7
Playing area:	Length of the netball court
Duration:	5-10 minutes
Outline:	Players covering the length of the court, approximately 3-5m apart. One player starts with the ball on the back line, 3m to the side of the line of players. The ball is passed in order down the line. Each player in the line returns the ball to the thrower who runs down the line. She retraces her path back to the beginning. The ball is passed to No.2 in the line who comes to the back line and repeats the activity. Meanwhile, No.1 runs behind the line to get to the end of the team.
Rules:	(1) After passing the ball each player in the line moves up a place. (2) A short pass must be used. (3) The running player must receive the ball over the back line at both ends of the team.

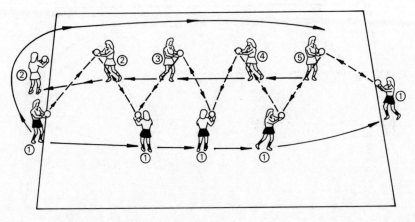

Game 46

Purpose:	Skills training (passing) and warming
No. of players:	In groups of 5 or 7
Playing area:	Length of the court
Duration:	5-10 minutes
Outline:	Starting as in Game 45. When No.1 gets to the opposite back line, she passes the ball to No.5 who passes it back down the line. When it gets to No.2 she repeats the activity.
Rules:	(1) Two-handed pass to be used by the player running down the team. (2) Chest pass to be used when coming down the team. (3) After receiving a pass from the moving player, that player moves down the line so that the activity can begin again, with No.2 standing behind the starting line and No.1 at the end of the line.
Variation:	The running player, when she gets to the end of the team, uses one pass to get the ball back to the beginning.

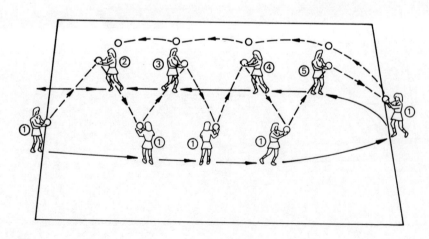

Game 47

Purpose:	Skills training (passing)
No. of players:	Teams of 5 or more
Playing area:	10m × 10m
Duration:	5-10 minutes
Outline:	Players in a circle with one player in the centre; one ball with the centre player and one with a circle player. The centre player passes the ball to the player next to the circle player with the other ball. The circle player passes to the centre player as soon as she has released her ball.
Rules:	(1) The centre player uses a two-handed pass. (2) After every circuit the centre player changes places (in turn) with a circle player. (3) Count the number of complete circuits achieved in 5 minutes.
Variations:	(1) Vary the pass used. (2) Change the direction in which the players throw.

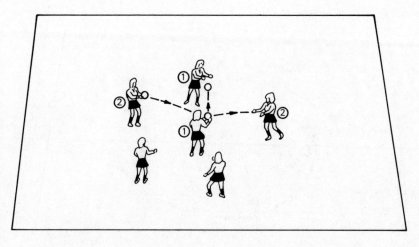

Game 48

Purpose:	Skills training (throwing)
No. of players:	Teams of 5 or more
Playing area:	10m × 10m
Duration:	3-5 minutes
Outline:	Players in a circle with one player in the centre with the ball. One circle player runs outside the circle and receives the ball between the next two players. She passes back to the centre and moves on to the next gap. This is repeated until she gets back to her original place. She then takes the centre player's place and passes to the next circle player. The centre player fills the gap.
Rules:	(1) The players use a chest pass. (2) Centre player uses a pivot. (3) Count the number of completed circuits.
Variation:	The running player must use a different pass from the one sent by the centre player.

Game 49

Purpose: Skills training (passing)
No. of players: Teams of 5 or more
Playing area: 10m × 10m
Duration: 5 minutes
Outline: As in Game 48 but players spaced so that one player is unable to touch the next player.
Rules: As in Game 48 but (1) the circle players may move sideways to intercept the pass to the moving player. (2) Count the number of successful circuits completed, i.e. with no interceptions. (3) If the ball is intercepted it is returned to the centre player. (4) The centre player uses any appropriate pass to avoid the defenders.

Game 50

Purpose:	Skills training and speed reaction
No. of players:	In teams of at least 8
Playing area:	10m × 10m
Duration:	3 minutes
Outline:	Six players in a circle; two players back-to-back in the centre, each with a ball. As in Game 48, but two players running round.
Rules:	(1) The first team to complete a full circuit, i.e. all players have been in the centre, are the winners. (2) The centre players use a pivot.
Variations:	(1) Vary the direction in which the players run. (2) Limit the pass used.
Remarks:	The players need to be relatively skilful.

Game 51

Purpose:	Skills training (throwing and catching)
No. of players:	In teams of 8 or more
Playing area:	10m × 10m
Duration:	5 minutes
Outline:	As in Game 50.
Rules:	(1) Centre players pass to circle players who remain stationary. The ball is returned to the centre and this is repeated until it gets back to the first players who keep the ball and change places with the centre players. (2) Two-handed pass to be used. (3) Count the number of complete circuits.
Variations:	Alter the pass and the direction in which the centre passes the ball around the circle.

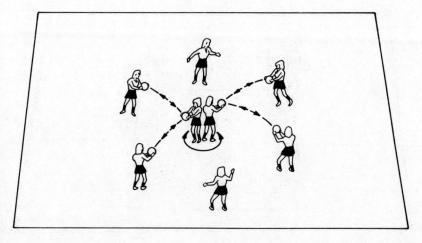

Game 52

Purpose:	Skills training (passing)
No. of players:	In groups of 3
Playing area:	5m × 5m approx.
Duration:	5 minutes
Outline:	Working on a square, the three players pass the ball, in order, to the player running into the free corner.
Rules:	(1) Players stand at corners of the square. (2) A chest pass to be used. (3) The ball travels on the lines of the square. (4) After returning to their original places, the players pass in the opposite direction. (5) Count the number of complete sequences.
Variations:	(1) Vary the pass, but it must be short and direct. (2) The game can be made more difficult if the player receiving the ball turns in the air or on landing, so that she faces the next player.
Remarks:	Timing is important in this game; the player has to move into the corner to receive the ball just as the thrower catches the ball.

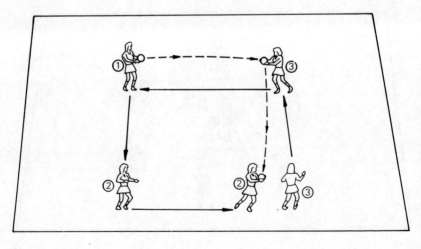

Game 53

Purpose:	Skills training (throwing)
No. of players:	Any number (individual work)
Playing area:	5m × 5m
Duration:	5 minutes
Outline:	This game requires a target, either marked on the wall or netting approximately 2m high. The target can be a square, approximately 35cm. A line should be marked approximately 5m from the target and 3m long. The player starts at the end of the line, aims at the target and retrieves the ball at the opposite end of the line. The player repeats the activity, arriving back at the starting position.
Rules:	(1) Feet must be behind the line. (2) Use an underarm pass when aiming. (3) A point is awarded for each successful hit. Winner is the player with the highest number of points.
Variations:	(1) Alter the pass for aiming – two-handed, shoulder. (2) Vary the footwork used when retrieving the ball, i.e. pivoting, turning in the air.

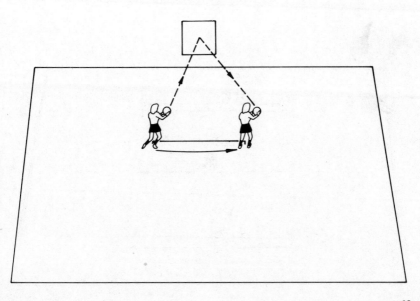

Game 54

Purpose:	Skills training (sideways interception)
No. of players:	In groups of three
Playing area:	10m × 5m approx.
Duration:	3-5 minutes
Outline:	Two players approximately 8m apart, facing each other on a line 5m long with the third player in the middle. The middle player tries to intercept the pass between the two players on the lines.
Rules:	(1) The middle player intercepts the pass from one player only. (2) She must stay in the middle of her area. (3) The players on the lines move right/left to receive the ball. (4) They must use a pass which doesn't go above shoulder level. (5) The defender scores a point for each interception.
Variations:	(1) The middle player may intercept passes coming from either player. (2) The players on the lines select any pass.

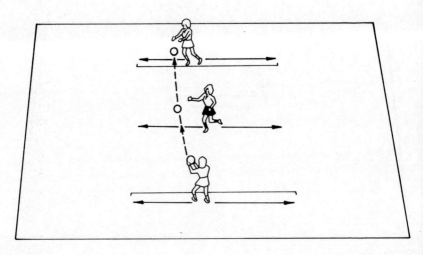

Game 55

Purpose:	Skills training (intercepting)
No. of players:	In groups of three
Playing area:	10m × 5m
Duration:	3-5 minutes
Outline:	As in Game 54, but the defending player starts from a set point. The line players throw and catch from one place.
Rules:	As in Game 54.

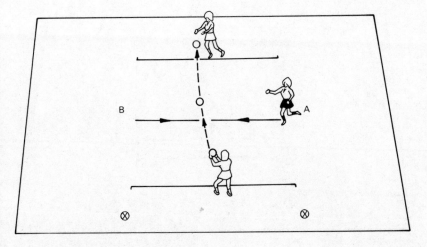

Game 56

Purpose: Skills training (space defending)
No. of players: In groups of 5
Playing area: 10m × 10m approx.
Duration: 3-5 minutes
Outline: Two players approximately 5m apart sideways, facing two other players 10m away. The extra player is in the middle of the four players and will be defending the two players behind her. Nos. 1 and 2 pass the ball between them and then pass to Nos. 4 and 3 trying to avoid the middle player.

Rules: (1) The defending player only intercepts the ball going to the players behind her. (2) Players No.1 and 2 may pass only to the player directly opposite them. (3) The defending player scores a point for a deflection and 2 points for an interception. (4) Count the number of points gained in 3 minutes.

Variation: The passing players vary the kind of pass used.

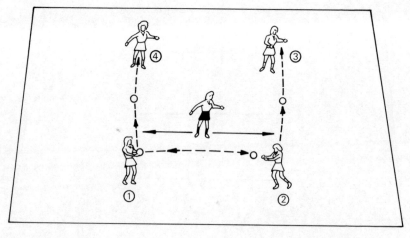

Game 57

Purpose:	Skills training and warming
No. of players:	In groups of three
Playing area:	10m × 5m
Duration:	3-5 minutes
Outline:	Two players approximately 2m apart passing the ball between one another, the third player in the middle trying to intercept.
Rules:	(1) The two outside players must remain still and pass only when the third player is in the middle. (2) The third player starts half way between the two players and moves back to intercept an overhead pass. She runs to the centre to intercept the return pass. (3) When the player intercepts she passes the ball to the nearest player, then runs to the centre. (4) Count the number of interceptions.
Variation:	Score 1 point for a deflection, 2 points for an interception.
Remarks:	The intercepting player should practise turning sideways as she moves backwards to intercept.

Game 58

Purpose:	Skills training (defending)
No. of players:	Groups of 4
Playing area:	10m × 5m approx.
Duration:	3-5 minutes
Outline:	Two players approximately 8m apart facing one another with a third player 3m to the side of one of them. The defending player, i.e. No.4, starts on a set mark (3m from the player with the ball). The defending player tries to intercept the pass from No.1 to No.2 and from No.1 to No.3.
Rules:	(1) The defender only intercepts passes from No.1. (2) The defender must return to the mark before trying to intercept. (3) The passing players must give the defender time to return to her mark before passing. (4) The ball is passed in the following order: 1 to 2, 2 to 1, 1 to 3, 3 to 1. (5) Passes between Nos. 1 and 2 should be shoulder passes; passes between Nos. 1 and 3 should be short.
Variations:	(1) Move No.3 to the other side or add another player (No.4) on No.1's free side. Throwing order with extra player: 1 to 2, 2 to 1, 1 to 3, 3 to 1, 1 to 2, 2 to 1, 1 to 4, 4 to 1.
Remarks:	No.1 must wait until the defender is near the mark before passing.

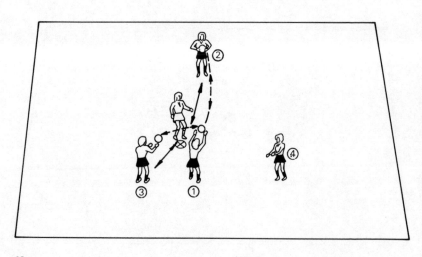

Game 59

Purpose: Skills training (defending)
No. of players: Groups of 5 or 7
Playing area: 10m × 10m
Duration: 5 minutes
Outline: As in Game 58, but the defending player tries to intercept only the overhead pass to No.2 and then marks No.1's throw to No.3. The defender returns to her mark. Players No.3 and 4 are marked by two additional players.

Rules: As in Game 58 except (1) No.3 must dodge to receive the pass from No.1; (2) No.4 must dodge to receive the pass from No.1.

Variations: (1) Nos. 3 and 4 use a change of direction dodge. (2) No.1 varies her pass so that she avoids the defence.

Game 60

Purpose:	Skills training (dodging and marking)
No. of players:	Two teams: one of 4, one of 3
Playing area:	10m × 10m
Duration:	5 minutes
Outline:	Team of 4 try to keep possession of the ball while the team of 3 try to intercept or force the other team into making an error. The organisation of the team is the same as in Game 58.
Rules:	(1) The attacking team (team of 4) must pass in the following way: 1 to 2, 2 to 1, then No. 1 has the choice of using either No.3 or No.4. (2) Each time the attacking team succeed in passing to Nos. 3 or 4 they score a point. (3) The three defenders are split as follows: one marks the pass to No.2 and No.1's throw to 3/4. The other two defenders mark Nos. 3 and 4 respectively. (4) The defenders score a point for a deflection and 2 points for an interception.
Variations:	Nos. 3 and 4 introduce a variety of dodges and score a point only if they use a different dodge each time.

Game 61

Purpose:	Skills training (space defending)
No. of players:	In groups of 3
Playing area:	A netball court
Duration:	5-10 minutes
Outline:	Each group of three attackers working individually, tries to get past lines of three players to the end of the court.
Rules:	(1) The defending lines of three work across a small area and they must not go into the next area. (2) The attackers may use any free space on the court to get past the other players. (3) No contact may be made. (4) As a player passes a defender, the defender moves forward into the next area. (5) When the defender gets to the front of the line she becomes an attacker and tries to get through the others.
Variations:	The three attackers work together to get through the defence. Points are scored if they get through successfully without making contact and going out of court.

71

Game 62

Purpose:	Skills training (interception)
No. of players:	Teams of 3
Playing area:	30m × 8m (half the court)
Duration:	5-10 minutes
Outline:	The court is divided lengthwise, i.e. from one goal post to the other. A team of three is in each third of their half of the court. The teams in the end thirds pass to one another trying to keep possession. The team in the middle try to intercept.
Rules:	(1) Players must remain in their area. (2) The middle team must make three interceptions before changing with one of the other teams. (3) The teams in the end thirds must vary their pass. (4) The end teams score a point each if they get four passes between them without an interception.
Variations:	(1) Set the type of pass. (2) The middle team stay in this position for a set number of minutes, and the number of interceptions made in that time is counted.
Remarks:	High pass encourages overhead interception, shoulder pass encourages sideways interception.

Game 63

Purpose:	Skills training (passing, man-to-man defending)
No. of players:	Teams of 3-4, plus 1 extra player
Playing area:	10m × 15m
Duration:	15 minutes
Outline:	The extra player in the centre circle. The teams pass the ball, scoring a point each time the player in the circle catches the ball.
Rules:	(1) The ball must be caught wholly in the circle. (2) The circle player passes to the team which threw the ball to her. (3) Highest number of passes in the given time. (4) Change the extra player at the end of the given time.
Variations:	(1) Limit the number of passes each team make before trying to score. (2) The passes must cover the whole area, i.e. the attacking players move to receive the ball.

Game 64

Purpose:	Skills training (throw-up)
No. of players:	In groups of 6
Playing area:	Any size
Duration:	3-5 minutes
Outline:	Group divided into three pairs, i.e. three against three. The game starts with a throw-up between one pair, then three passes are made by the team with the ball.
Rules:	(1) Pairs numbered 1, 2 and 3. (2) One of the No.1 players takes a throw-up between the No.2 pair. The winner passes to her team's No.3 then on to No.1 and finally to No.2.(3) No.2 then takes a throw-up between the No.3s and so on. (4) Each player takes a throw-up in turn. (5) One point is scored for gaining the ball from a throw-up and another point if the team succeed in passing the ball as directed. (6) If intercepted by the opposing team, the intercepting player starts the game with a throw-up between the next pair of players, e.g. No.3 intercepts and takes a throw-up between the two No.1s.

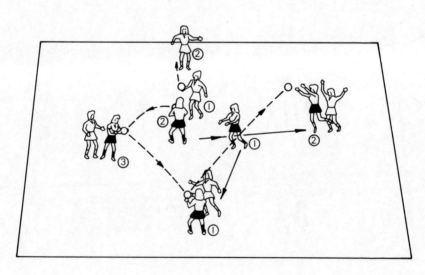

Game 65

Purpose:	Skills training (defensive work)
No. of players:	Two teams of 7
Playing area:	Netball court
Duration:	15 minutes
Outline:	A normal game of netball but with emphasis on the defending aspect.
Rules:	(1) Points can be scored by the defending team – 1 point for a deflection, 2 points for an interception, 1 point for making an opponent hold the ball for 3 seconds. (2) The points are added to the number of goals scored by each team.
Variation:	The defending team lose a point if they allow their opponents to score a goal.
Remarks:	Many practices should be geared to man-to-man defending.

Game 66

Purpose:	Tactical training
No. of players:	Teams of 3
Playing area:	A third of the court
Duration:	5 minutes
Outline:	As in Game 44, but players trying to get the ball from one line to the opposite line, i.e. back line to third line, between two centre-third lines.
Rules:	(1) Passes must be in order 1 to 2, 2 to 3, etc. (2) The last pass must be caught over the line to score a point. (3) Passes must go to the called player.
Variations:	(1) Each player must receive the ball at least once before scoring a point. (2) There must be four passes before a team score a point. (3) Limit (a) the dodge, (b) the pass.
Remarks:	The coach may call the number of the player to receive the pass.

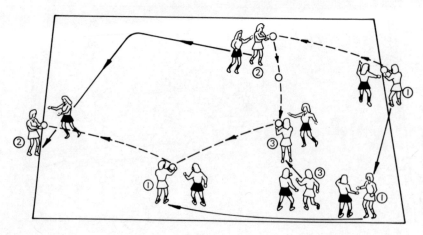

Game 67

Purpose:	Tactical training (timing)
No. of players:	In teams of 4
Playing area:	5m × 10m
Duration:	3-5 minutes
Outline:	Players in pairs, approximately 8m apart standing on a line. No.1 passes to No.2 (beside her) who moves into the playing area to receive the ball. Player No.4 is marked by No.3. As No.2 receives the ball No.4 dodges to receive the pass. This is repeated with each player changing position, i.e. Nos. 4 and 3 become thrower and receiver. No.3 then passes to No.1 (who is marked by No.2).
Rules:	(1) The first pass must be a shoulder pass; the second one an underarm pass. (2) The dodge should be a sprint dodge.
Variations:	Vary (a) the pass, (b) the dodge.
Remarks:	Emphasize the correct timing of the attacking player who receives the second pass.

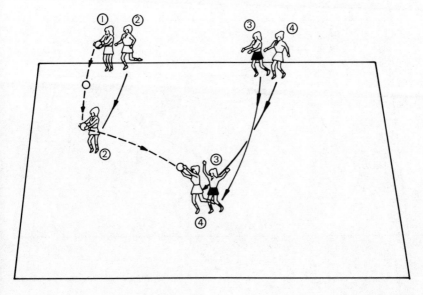

Game 68

Purpose:	Tactical training (timing)
No. of players:	5 players, divided 3:2
Playing area:	15m × 10m
Duration:	5 minutes
Outline:	One player, with the ball, outside the playing area; the others spaced out two against two. The ball is passed to one of the thrower's team, who passes to the third member of the team. Then the defending team become the attackers and the other team defend.
Rules:	(1) A sprint dodge must be used. (2) The players aim to get as near to the opposite line as possible in the two moves. (3) Score 1 point for two successful passes from the line. (4) The player behind the line does not enter the playing area.
Variations:	(1) Change the method of dodging. (2) Limit the pass used. (3) Make the unmarked player receive the third pass behind the opposite line.
Remarks:	The timing of the dodge is important. The dodge used will depend on the timing of the attacking player.

Game 69

Purpose:	Tactical training
No. of players:	Two teams of 5
Playing area:	A third of the court
Duration:	5-10 minutes
Outline:	Both teams try to keep possession of the ball within the playing area.
Rules:	(1) Each player is numbered and they must pass in order. (2) One point is scored every time the ball arrives at the starting player. (3) The players are free to move within their area.
Variations:	(1) Count the number of passes made consecutively. (2) Players must use a sequence of different passes, i.e. one short followed by two long, etc. (3) Each player must receive the ball at least once to score a point.

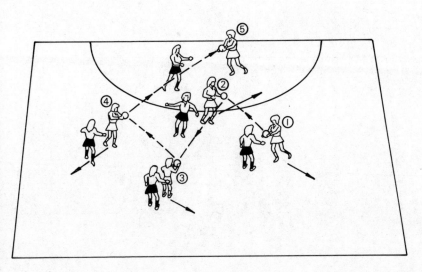

Game 70

Purpose:	Tactical and stamina training
No. of players:	Two teams of 5
Playing area:	A third of the court
Duration:	10 minutes
Outline:	Both teams try to score as many goals as possible in 10 minutes.
Rules:	(1) Both teams shoot into the same goal. (2) Only two players from each team are allowed to go into the circle to shoot. (3) The game starts on the third line. (4) Teams must make five passes before they can shoot. (5) Players must be in the circle in order to shoot. (6) Only one shot is allowed after five passes. (7) After a missed shot, the team retrieving the ball continue the game. (8) After a goal has been scored, the opposite team start the game from the third line.
Variations:	(1) Every player must receive the ball at least once before shooting. (2) On an interception, the team must play the ball back to the third line before heading back to the goal.

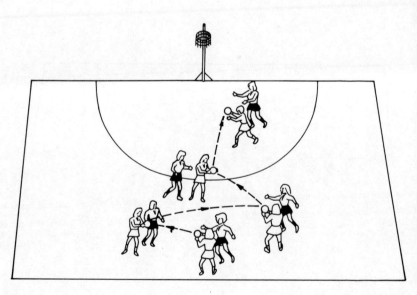

Game 71

Purpose:	Tactical and spatial training and warming up
No. of players:	In groups of three
Playing area:	Any size
Duration:	3 minutes
Outline:	The three players in a triangular formation. Each player moves between the other two players to receive the ball. All players progress down the court.
Rules:	(1) Players use a short pass. (2) The three players score a point if they succeed in getting the ball to the end of the area.
Variation:	The team of three try to do this practice but with defender.

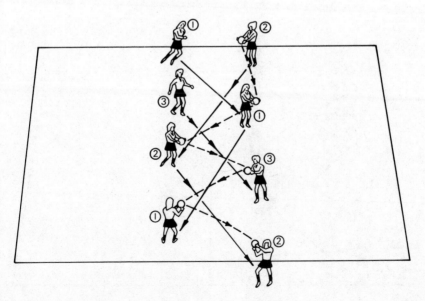

Game 72

Purpose:	Tactical and spatial training
No. of players:	In twos
Playing area:	10m × 8m
Duration:	3-5 minutes
Outline:	The players start 5m apart, side by side. They aim to receive the ball on the move and at a right angle to one another. They use a straight, direct pass.
Rules:	(1) The players work on a square. (2) The ball travels along the sides of the square. (3) The players sprint across the square, i.e. on the diagonal. (4) Each player waits to sprint to the corner of the square until her partner has turned into the centre. (5) Count the number of successful passes.
Remarks:	When the players become more skilful, the timing of the throw can be speeded up. Also the player catching the ball can turn to face the centre on landing.

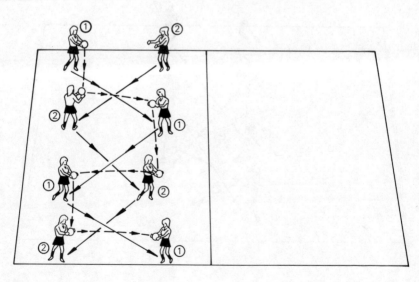

Game 73

Purpose:	Tactical training
No. of players:	In twos
Playing area:	Approx. 8m × 8m
Duration:	3-5 minutes
Outline:	As in Game 72, players working in a square. Players receiving the ball on a straight line, i.e. the lines of the square.
Rules:	(1) The player with the ball (No.1) starts at the corner of the square. The other player (No.2) starts in the middle of the square, facing the player with the ball. (2) No.2 may receive the ball in either the right- or left-hand corner. (3) Immediately the thrower has released the ball, she runs into the centre and faces the other player. (4) The thrower must wait until the other player is in the centre before passing. (5) The players with the highest number of successful passes in the given time are the winners.
Variations:	(1) Add an opposing team. (2) Add Game 72, i.e. the players get the ball from one line to the opposite line; they have the choice of a sprint to one corner of the square, thus progressing immediately down the court, or sprinting to the corner away from the line.

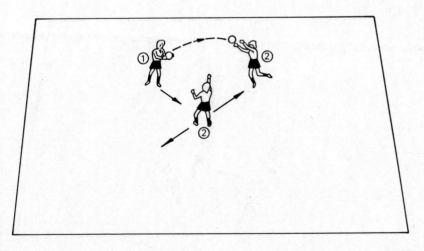

Game 74

Purpose:	Tactical and spatial training and warming up
No. of players:	In groups of three
Playing area:	10m × 10m
Duration:	5-10 minutes
Outline:	Players spaced in the area, the thrower passing towards the second player but the third player running in to catch the ball. The other player fills the gap left by the receiver.
Rules:	(1) The thrower has free choice of which player she throws to. (2) After throwing, the player stays still. (3) Use a variety of passes, i.e. correct selection for the distance to be thrown. (4) Count the number of successful passes in the set time.
Variations:	(1) Limit the type of pass used. (2) Repeat the activity with opposition. When the ball is intercepted the team repeat the same exercise.

Game 75

Purpose:	Tactical training for circle players
No. of players:	Teams of 3-4
Playing area:	A third of the court
Duration:	10 minutes
Outline:	Team A – two shooters and one (or two) centre court player(s). Team B – two defences and one (or two) centre court player(s). The attacking team try to keep possession of the ball by moving to receive the pass and ultimately score a goal.
Rules:	(1) The centre court player starts with the ball, just inside the centre third. (2) If the ball is intercepted, the defending team pass the ball until they get it into the centre third. (3) Method of scoring: Attacks – (a) six passes before shooting; (b) every player receives the ball once; Defences – (a) six passes must be made before scoring; (b) all players must receive the ball once. (4) The game is re-started after a goal/point has been scored by a pass in the centre third by the non-scoring team.

Game 76

Purpose:	Tactical and stamina training
No. of players:	Two teams of 8
Playing area:	A netball court
Duration:	15-20 minutes
Outline:	Teams are divided into five and three, the group of five in the end thirds and the group of three in the centre third. (The centre third is divided in half through the centre circle.) Each end group tries to get the ball to the remainder of the team, by passing through the opposition.
Rules:	(1) Players must remain in their own area. (2) One point for a successful pass and interception. (3) The game starts with a throw-up between two players in the centre area.
Variations:	(1) Limit the pass, i.e. no pass must be below waist level. (2) Introduce another ball.

Game 77

Purpose:	Tactical and stamina training
No. of players:	Teams of 4
Playing area:	A third of the court
Duration:	3-5 minutes
Outline:	Three players from one team plus one from the opposition space out in half the playing area. The attacking members of the team pass the ball between them until they are able to pass to their player in the other area.
Rules:	(1) Three passes at least, must be made before trying to pass to the fourth player. (2) Score 1 point for a successful pass.
Variations:	(1) Allow any number of passes but introduce a set pass. (2) The player intercepting scores a point for her team.

Game 78

Purpose:	Tactical training
No. of players:	Teams of 3
Playing area:	A netball court
Duration:	5-10 minutes
Outline:	One team start behind the goal line with the ball and pass between themselves, aiming to get the ball to the opposite goal line. Three other teams are defending a third of the court each; they try to break the attacking team's move down, i.e. by (a) making them pass inaccurately; (b) intercepting a pass.
Rules:	(1) The personal contact and obstruction rules should be very carefully enforced. (2) If the defender intercepts she scores one point, but returns the ball to the attackers who continue on to the next three defenders. (3) As the attacking three move on to the next third, the three defenders move on to the next third and eventually become the attacking three. (4) The defending three may not go out of their area when defending. (5) The attackers may move freely.

Game 79

Purpose:	Tactical training
No. of players:	Two teams of 5
Playing area:	10m × 15m
Duration:	10 minutes
Outline:	The teams are divided into two attackers, two defenders and one centre. Divide the area into thirds, with a goal post at each end. Two attackers in one end third, two defenders in the other end third, and the centre in the middle third. The defending players aim to get the ball to their attacking players.
Rules:	(1) Defending players start with the ball. (2) The first pass must go to the other defender, then to the centre player, who passes to either of the attackers. (3) Both attacking players must receive the ball before they can shoot. (4) The last pass must be caught in the circle. (5) Only one attacker allowed in the circle at any one time. (6) Count the number of goals scored. (7) Defenders start the game again after a goal.
Variations:	(1) Pairs must have three passes in their own area before passing to the centre player. (2) Every player must receive the ball before the team may shoot, i.e. it can go from defender to attacker to centre.

DEFENDERS

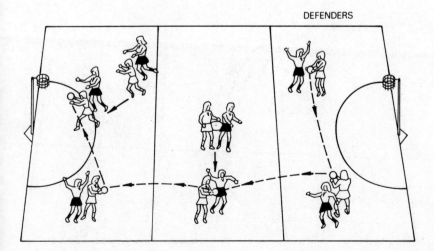

Game 80

Purpose:	Tactical training for centre court players (spacing)
No. of players:	Teams of 5
Playing area:	Netball court
Duration:	15 minutes
Outline:	Teams consist of one attacking player, three centre players, and one defender. Defending and attacking players in opposite end thirds. The three centre players in the centre third. The defending player starts with the ball and every member of the team must receive the ball, finishing in the attacking third.
Rules:	(1) All the centre players must receive the pass in the centre area before passing to the attacking player. (2) Score 1 point for each successful pass to the attacking player.
Variations:	(1) After all centre players have received the ball, one of them may go into the attacking third for another pass before passing to the attacking player, who lands in the circle. She then shoots. (2) One centre player may go into the defenders' third to receive a pass, then the game continues. (3) Nos. 1 and 2 can both be used as well as using all three centre players in the centre third. (4) As in (2) but only two passes in the centre third.

Game 81

Purpose:	Tactical training
No. of players:	Teams of 9
Playing area:	A netball court
Duration:	10-15 minutes
Outline:	The team divided into three defenders, three centre court players, and three attackers, i.e. GK, GD, WD; WA, C, WD; and WA, GA, GS. Each trio is in its respective third. The groups of three pass the ball from the beginning of their third to the edge of the next. Then they pass into the next third, and so on to the end third.
Rules:	(1) The ball starts behind the goal line with a defender. (2) The groups must stay in their own third. (3) Each group numbered 1-3. (4) When the ball gets to the end of one third the player with the ball calls a number and that player in the next third moves to receive the pass. (5) Players must receive the ball at least once in their own third before passing to the next third.
Variations:	(1) Alter the number of passes in each area. (2) No calling, the player with the ball selects the most appropriate player in the next third. (3) The teams have opponents who try to intercept. (4) The groups of three are not given positions, so that when the opposition intercept the ball, they are working to get the ball to the same end of the court, i.e. shooting into the same goal.

91

Game 82

Purpose:	Reaction training
No. of players:	In groups of 3
Playing area:	10m × 5m approx.
Duration:	5 minutes
Outline:	The three players start side by side behind a line, the middle one has the ball. She throws the ball ahead of her (not more than 5m). The other players chase the ball, pick it up and return it to the thrower. Both return to the starting line.
Rules:	(1) Chasing players must have both feet behind the line before they go for the next pass. (2) The thrower passes the ball as soon as the players are over the line. (3) The thrower may toss, bounce, pass the ball how she wishes. (4) The chasing players get the ball as quickly as possible. Not more than two touches on the ground before catching the ball. (5) The player scores a point each time she is successful.
Variations:	(1) The player who fails to get the ball, marks the return pass to the thrower. (Score 1 point if she touches the pass.) (2) The thrower may put the ball in front or behind the line (make sure there is sufficient space in both areas).

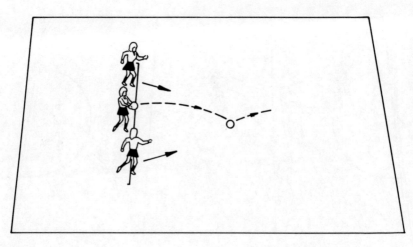

Game 83

Purpose:	Reaction training and skills practice (shooting)
No. of players:	In groups of three
Playing area:	10m × 8m with a goal post
Duration:	5 minutes
Outline:	As in Game 82 but the three players face towards the goal. The two players chasing the ball finish in the circle and the one who retrieves the ball shoots. Both players go for the rebound, then pass back to the thrower. The chasing players are aiming to get as many goals as possible.
Rules:	As in Game 82. (1) The shooters must return to their positions beside the thrower before the ball is released again. (2) The thrower varies her pass but makes sure it will reach the circle. (3) After throwing the ball for the shooter, the thrower runs into a different space outside the circle. (4) All players change position after a given time.
Variation:	The player who fails to get the ball in the circle, becomes the defence and marks the shot.

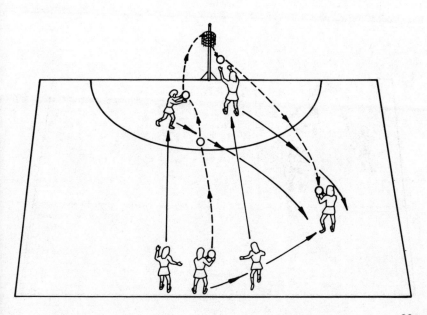

Game 84

Purpose:	Reaction training
No. of players:	In twos
Playing area:	5m × 5m
Duration:	3-5 minutes
Outline:	The players face one another. One player throws the ball into the area and places it so that the other player finds it difficult to catch.
Rules:	(1) The ball may be thrown or tossed but must be kept above waist level. (2) The ball must land in the area. (3) If the thrower passes the ball out of the area her opponent scores a point. (4) If the ball touches the ground the thrower scores a point.
Remarks:	Players must re-position after releasing the ball and keep on their toes. Have hands ready to catch.

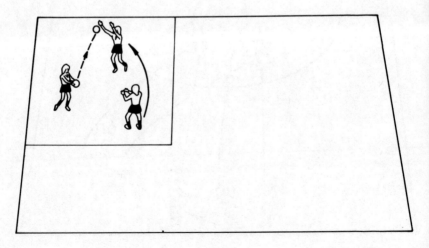

Game 85

Purpose:	Reaction training
No. of players:	In twos
Playing area:	10m × 10m
Duration:	5 minutes
Outline:	The square is divided in half diagonally. In each half there are three circles evenly distributed. Each player must catch the ball in one of the circles.
Rules:	(1) The players are free to move in their own area. (2) The ball must be thrown above waist level. (3) A player must not make contact with the ground outside the circle while she has the ball. (4) If the ball lands outside the area, the opponent gains a point. (5) If the player fails to catch the ball, her opponent gains a point.
Variations (for skilful players):	(1) Limit how the players land in the circle. (2) Allow the ball to go lower than the waist but not below the knees.

Game 86

Purpose:	Reaction training
No. of players:	In groups of 2 or 4
Playing area:	5m × 5m
Duration:	5 minutes
Outline:	Players side by side facing the wall (or netting) (approximately 5m from the wall). A line/mark on the wall. One player throws the ball to hit the wall above the line. The other player sprints to catch the ball before it touches the ground. The

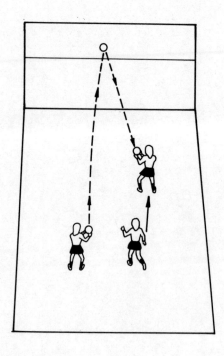

ball is taken alternately and players try to get the rebound as many times as possible.

Rules: (1) The thrower tries to throw the ball so that the rebound comes off at a difficult angle and speed for the catcher. (2) If playing two against two, the same rules apply but after throwing the ball each player goes behind her partner.

Variation: The retrieving player alters her starting position, i.e. instead of standing facing the wall she may kneel, sit, back to the wall, etc.

Game 87

Purpose:	Reaction training
No. of players:	In teams of 3-7
Playing area:	Any size
Duration:	3-5 minutes
Outline:	Players numbered 1-7 and in a circle. The players should be unable to touch one another across the circle. One player tosses or throws the ball in the air in the circle area and calls a number. The player called must catch the ball before it hits the ground.
Rules:	(1) The ball must not touch the ground. (2) The catcher releases the ball immediately she has caught it and calls another number. (3) After releasing the ball the thrower moves out to join the circle again. (4) The catcher may run or jump to catch the ball.
Variations:	(1) Widen the size of the circle. (2) Throw the ball into different areas of the circle to make it more difficult for the catcher.

Game 88

Purpose:	Reaction and skills training (throw-up and timing)
No. of players:	Groups of 3
Playing area:	Any size
Duration:	3 minutes
Outline:	In threes, two players facing one another (1m apart). The third player takes the throw-up and then moves right or left to receive a pass from the player gaining the ball from the throw-up.
Rules:	(1) Players must obey all the rules concerned with the throw-up. (2) Count the number of times a player is successful in getting the ball.
Variation:	The player putting in the ball should change sides.

Game 89

Purpose:	Reaction training
No. of players:	Two teams of 5
Playing area:	20m × 15m
Duration:	5-10 minutes
Outline:	The area divided in half. Both teams defend the space in their area and try to prevent any balls touching the ground.
Rules:	(1) Teams have two netballs each. (2) Teams throw the balls freely into their opponents' area. (3) If a ball hits the ground, the team which threw it score a point. (4) The team lose a point if the ball lands outside the area without touching the ground inside it.
Variations:	(1) Limit the pass used. (2) Add another ball.

Game 90

Purpose:	Supplementary game
No. of players:	Two teams of 9-10
Playing area:	A netball court
Duration:	15-20 minutes
Outline:	Two teams. Seven players start in the normal playing positions and play a normal game of netball. When a goal is scored one player drops out and a new player comes in. Teams try to be the first to get their players back to their original positions.
Rules:	(1) Only the scoring team bring in a new player. (2) The player dropping out is always the GK. (3) The players move on in the following order: WD to C, C to GA, GA to GS, GS to WA, WA to GD, GD to GK, and GK out. The new player always comes in as WD.
Variation:	The extra players can be given a task to perform, e.g. running, skipping, ball skills, etc. They can gain extra points for their team, depending on the number of times they complete their task.

Game 91

Purpose:	Supplementary game (space marking)
No. of players:	Any number
Playing area:	A netball court
Duration:	15-20 minutes
Outline:	Players divided into two equal teams. The end third of the court is a 'safe zone'. The first team cover the rest of the court and try to prevent the attacking team getting through to the 'safe zone'. The attacking team line up on the goal line. Each player catches the ball thrown by a defender towards her, then she throws the ball anywhere in the playing area. Once she has thrown the ball, the attacker runs to the 'safe zone' and back to the beginning again, if possible. Then the next player comes in.
Rules:	(1) One defender is the thrower and stays on one spot to throw. (2) The defender must not run with the ball. (3) The ball can be passed freely

among the defenders. (4) The defenders may move freely in the area so that they can make it more difficult for the attacker to get through (however, they must obey the obstruction and contact rules). (5) The attacker is out if a defender can hit her with the ball on the legs. (6) If the defender who throws to the other team is back in position with the ball, the attacker may not return to the start, unless she is in the playing area on her return run. (7) Once the attacker is in the 'safe zone' she cannot be out. She may remain in this area as long as she likes, but the attacking team must ensure that they have a player on the goal line. (8) The attackers score a point if they get into the 'safe zone' without being hit and another point if they return to the goal line safely. (9) When all the team are out, they change over.

Remarks: A smaller or softer ball may be used instead of a standard-size netball.

Game 92

Purpose:	Supplementary game (stamina training)
No. of players:	Two teams of 7
Playing area:	Netball court
Duration:	5-10 minutes
Outline:	The court is divided in half through the centre circle. The teams (A and B) each cover their area, i.e. half the court. Team A start with the ball behind the goal line. The player throws the ball into her opponent's half then runs to the centre circle, goes round it and returns to the start. Team B field the ball. The rest of the team form a line behind her and each player receives the ball. The team A player is trying to beat the ball to the end of the line.
Rules:	(1) Team B: Use a chest pass to each player. The last player calls 'stop' as she catches the ball. If they beat the runner they score a point. (2) Team A: The ball must land in the playing area, i.e. the netball court. A point is scored if the runner gets over the starting line before the ball gets to the last player in the opposition.
Variation:	All team A follow the thrower round the circle and finish behind the back line.

Game 93

Purpose:	Supplementary game (skills training in a warming activity)
No. of players:	Two teams of 3 or 5
Playing area:	10m × 15m
Duration:	10 minutes
Outline:	One skittle in a circle (3m diameter) in the middle of the area. Teams try to knock down the skittle.
Rules:	(1) The defending team may not enter the circle but can defend it from outside. (2) Only two defenders allowed around the skittle at one time. (3) The attacking team must make three passes before aiming at the skittle.
Variations:	Use different methods of defending: (1) man-to-man; (2) marking the space and defending the skittle.

Game 94

Purpose:	Supplementary game
No. of players:	Teams of 7
Playing area:	A netball court
Duration:	15-20 minutes
Outline:	Three skittles arranged in each circle. Teams defend one circle each and try to knock down their opponents' skittles. Teams may position their skittles freely in their circle.
Rules:	(1) Teams are free to move anywhere on the court. (2) The game starts with a throw-up in the centre circle. (3) No team may knock a skittle down from a back line throw-in. (4) The skittles remain down. The first team to get all their opponents' skittles down are the winners.

Game 95

Purpose: Supplementary game utilizing extra players
No. of players: 10 or more
Playing area: A netball court
Duration: 10 minutes
Outline: A normal game, with the extra players outside the court, evenly distributed on each side. The extra players may be used in general play to get the ball down the court.
Rules: (1) As in a normal game. (2) After two goals have been scored, a side-line player from each team changes with a court player. (3) The line players may be defended by a court player, who must remain on the court.

Game 96

Purpose:	Supplementary game
No. of players:	Teams of 7 or more
Playing area:	Any size, i.e. 1, 2 or 3 netball courts
Duration:	15-20 minutes
Outline:	Teams space themselves out in half the playing area. The team pass the ball between themselves trying to get to the opposite goal line and score a goal by shooting.
Rules:	(1) Players may move freely over the whole area (no offside rule). (2) Players may run with the ball. (3) If a defending player touches the player in possession of the ball, she must release it immediately. She may not play the ball again until it has been touched by another player. (4)

The game is started by a throw-up in the centre. This rule applies after a goal has been scored. (5) After a missed shot, the game continues with the team who retrieve the ball. (6) A shot may be made from anywhere.

Variations: (1) If playing without a post, e.g. on a field, a goal is scored by a player putting the ball down over the goal line. (2) No forward pass may be made. (3) If playing on more than one netball court, the team may shoot into any post along their goal line. (4) After the initial start, the game is continuous, i.e. after a goal the opposite team start with a throw-in behind the nearest line.

Remarks: Players should anticipate and learn to pass before being 'touched'. The rest of the team move to assist the player with the ball.